5/11 ⑨

Healthy Eating

Milk and Cheese

Nancy Dickmann

Heinemann Library
Chicago, Illinois

S0-ADE-763

www.heinemannraintree.com
Visit our website to find out
more information about
Heinemann-Raintree books.

To order:

☎ Phone 888-454-2279

🖥 Visit www.heinemannraintree.com
to browse our catalog and order online.

©2010 Heinemann Library
an imprint of Capstone Global Library, LLC
Chicago, Illinois

All rights reserved. No part of this publication may be reproduced or
transmitted in any form or by any means, electronic or mechanical,
including photocopying, recording, taping, or any information storage
and retrieval system, without permission in writing from the publisher.

Edited by Siân Smith, Nancy Dickmann, and Rebecca Rissman
Designed by Joanna Hinton-Malivoire
Original Illustrations © Capstone Global Library Ltd 2010
Illustrated by Tony Wilson
Picture research by Elizabeth Alexander
Production by Victoria Fitzgerald
Originated by Capstone Global Library Ltd
Printed and bound in China by South China Printing Company Ltd

ISBN 978-1-4329-3982-3
14 13 12 11 10
10 9 8 7 6 5 4 3 2 1

Library of Congress Cataloging-in-Publication Data

Dickmann, Nancy.
 Milk and cheese / Nancy Dickmann.
   p. cm. -- (Healthy eating)
 Includes bibliographical references and index.
 ISBN 978-1-4329-3982-3 (hc) -- ISBN 978-1-4329-3989-2 (pb) 1. Dairy
products in human nutrition--Juvenile literature. 2. Milk in human nutrition-
-Juvenile literature. I. Title.
 QP144.M54D53 2011
 613.2'6--dc22
                         2009045483

Acknowledgements
We would like to thank the following for permission to reproduce
photographs: © Capstone Publishers p.**22** (Karon Dubke); Alamy p.**15** (©
Cultura); Corbis pp.**18**, **23 bottom** (© Bernd Vogel), **21** (© moodboard);
Getty Images pp.**7** (Gavriel Jecan/The Image Bank), **19** (Dave King/Dorling
Kindersley); Getty Images/Digital Vision p.**14** (Christopher Robbins);
iStockphoto pp.**20**, **13** (© Rosemarie Gearhart), p**23 top** (© Mark Hatfield);
Photolibrary pp.**5** (Hans Huber/Westend61), **8** (Maximilian Stock LTD/
Phototake Science), **11** (Willy De L'Horme/Photononstop), **12** (Kablonk!),
16 (Banana Stock); Shutterstock pp.**4** (© Chepko Danil Vitalevich), **6** (©
Viorel Sima), **9** (© Morgan Lane Photography), **10** (© matka_Wariatka);
USDA Center for Nutrition Policy and Promotion p.**17**.

Front cover photograph of milk and dairy products reproduced with
permission of © Capstone Publishers (Karon Dubke). Back cover photograph
reproduced with permission of Shutterstock (© Viorel Sima).

We would like to thank Dr Sarah Schenker for her invaluable help in the
preparation of this book.

Every effort has been made to contact copyright holders of material
reproduced in this book. Any omissions will be rectified in subsequent
printings if notice is given to the publishers.

Contents

R0431467679

What Is Milk?

Milk is a drink that is made by some animals.

Drinking milk helps keep us healthy.

Most of our milk comes from cows.

goats

Some of our milk comes from goats.

Food from Milk

cheese

Milk can be made into other foods.

These foods are called dairy foods.

Cheese is made from milk.

Yogurt is made from milk.

How Milk Helps Us

Milk and dairy foods help to build strong bones.

Milk and dairy foods help to build strong teeth.

Milk and dairy foods help your body to grow.

Milk and dairy foods help to keep your blood healthy.

Healthy Eating

We need to eat different kinds of
food each day.

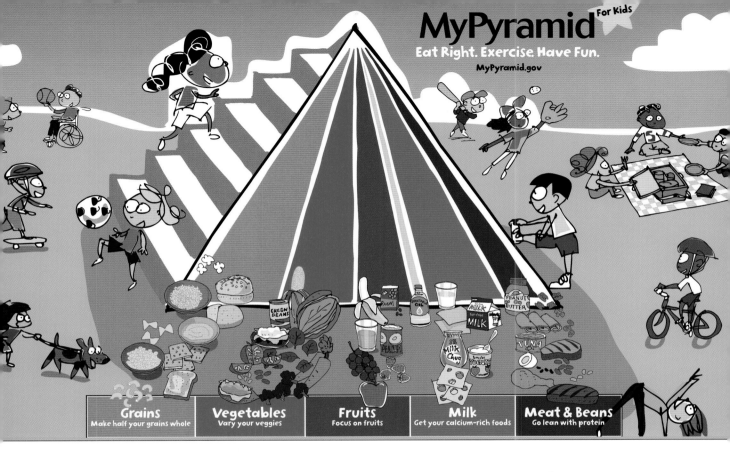

Grains
Make half your grains whole

Vegetables
Vary your veggies

Fruits
Focus on fruits

Milk
Get your calcium-rich foods

Meat & Beans
Go lean with protein

The food pyramid tells us to eat foods from each food group.

cheese

Some dairy foods have a lot of fat.

You should only eat a little of these foods.

We eat milk and dairy foods to stay healthy.

We eat milk and dairy foods because they taste good!

Find the Dairy Food

Here is a healthy dinner. Can you find two foods made from milk?

Answer on page 24

Picture Glossary

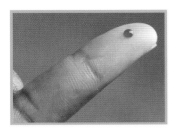 **blood** red liquid inside your body. Blood takes food and air to all your body parts.

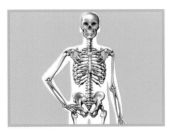 **bones** you have bones inside your body. Bones are strong and hard. They help to keep your body up.

 **fat** oily thing in some foods. Your body uses fat to keep warm. Eating too much fat is bad for your body.

Index

Answer to quiz on page 22: The cheese and the yogurt are made from milk.

Notes for parents and teachers

Before reading

Explain that we need to eat a range of different foods to stay healthy. Splitting foods into different groups can help us understand how much food we should eat from each group. Introduce the milk food group of the food pyramid on page 17. These foods give us calcium, which helps build strong teeth and bones. Explain that some people are allergic to milk and dairy products. They can get the calcium they need through special foods such as soy milk, which is made from soy beans.

After reading

- Brainstorm different dairy foods as a class. Explain that some dairy foods are high in fat and we need to be careful not to eat too much of these.
- Show how milk can be turned into butter. Fill a clear, lidded jar half full with heavy cream. Take turns shaking the jar. After about 20–30 minutes a lump of butter should form along with a liquid. Pour the liquid buttermilk into a separate container and wash the butter under cold water until the water runs clear. Taste the butter on whole grain bread or crackers.
- Help the children to make posters telling people to try milk and dairy foods. Use the posters to show why we need milk and dairy foods to help us build strong teeth and bones and to stay healthy.